P9-CLO-444

Reach deep down
to find the sunlight
within you.

This book of escape and transformation
belongs to:

_____   _____
YOUR NAME   DATE

Doodles
& Daydreams

Your passport for becoming an escape artist

BILL ZIMMERMAN
drawings by Tom Bloom

Gibbs Smith, Publisher

TO ENRICH AND INSPIRE HUMANKIND

Salt Lake City | Charleston | Santa Fe | Santa Barbara

First Edition
11 10 09 08 07   5 4 3 2 1

Published by
Gibbs Smith, Publisher
P.O. Box 667
Layton, Utah 84041

Orders: 1.800.835.4993
www.gibbs-smith.com

Book Design and Connect-the-Dots drawings by Eileen Berasi
Printed and bound in Korea

Library of Congress Control Number: 2005933700
ISBN 13: 978-1-4236-0152-4
ISBN 10: 1-4236-0152-1

You can see Bill Zimmerman's other work at his Web sites:
www.billztreasurechest.com and
www.makebeliefscomix.com

Dedicated to three special people
who opened up the world to me:
my elementary school teacher
Amelia R. DiNallo, who day after day
unselfishly spent hours after school
patiently showing me how to sound out
words and read; to the neighborhood
librarian, who read amazing stories to all
the children and made me want to read
every book in the place; and to my
cousin Ruth, who by her example gave a
young boy hope that there was a
wider world out there that he might
one day enter.

> *"Children, if you are tired, keep going;*
> *if you are scared, keep going;*
> *if you are hungry, keep going;*
> *if you want to taste freedom, keep going."*
>
> —Harriet Tubman, a former slave

It is said that in Africa and Asia farmers tame a wild elephant for work by tying one end of a rope to one of its feet and the other end to a banyan tree. Now this large tree's roots grow deep into the earth, making it impossible for the elephant to yank the tree from the ground and run away. In time, the elephant, feeling the tug of the rope, learns to stay in place. Then, the farmer can take the elephant out to work and keep it from running away by tying the rope on its foot to a small wooden stake in the ground. Feeling once again the tug of the rope, the elephant remains in place. It doesn't try to escape.

There is something to be learned here. How often do we allow ourselves to surrender our freedom because of force of habit or lack of imagination? Only by thinking imaginatively can we escape and be free once again.

Contents

7

8 6 5

9

2

3

end
1*

Complete your first connect-the-dots on this page!

Read
This Book
to Plot
Your Escape

W hen we think of
escape artists, we often think of Harry Houdini
submerged in a water tank and bound with chains
he must break before he runs out of oxygen and
drowns. But there are other kinds of escape artists, too—you included.

Take writers and artists, for example—most are
deliberate escape artists. They sit quietly for
hours at a table or easel, shutting off one world
to enter a new one of their own making.

Through their imaginations, they build castles in the sky, climb tall mountains, and soar among clouds. They're never at a loss for adventure  and always succeed. Failure has no admittance. For artists, the world of imagination is one in which they find sustenance and regain their strength. Imagination is what allows them to break the bindings that restrict their souls.

Here's where you come in. As this book will show you, when you really think about it, each of us is a little like Houdini, capable of freeing ourselves from the shackles we wear. Each of us has the inherent power to transport ourselves out of our straitjacketed misery into a better world. Escape then becomes a matter of attitude, of imagination, and of the capacity to dream and hope—we truly do hold the keys to our own locks. Simply put, great escape artists are transformers—they make good out of bad.

When, for example, we are trapped in our
commuter trains or cars, we can escape by
allowing our innermost fantasies to transform
what we see out the window. Instead of long lines
of stalled cars or telephone poles, we see a paradise kissed by oceans or a lush countryside
beckoning to us. Through our escapes, our
hearts talk to us at those
moments. We feel like we are
swimming with dolphins.

When we are ill and lie in
our beds struggling to heal
and recover, we try to visualize
what it would feel like to be healed and healthy,
and these imaginative moments ease our pain
and help us begin our recovery.

I think that I have always been an escape artist.
As a boy when all the screaming, the yelling, and
fighting at home got to me, I would retreat in
silence to a safer place—my imagination.

There, I could fly and be aware of the beauty in the universe. There, my soul found refuge and comfort. No fighting was allowed. I was always comfortable in the world of my imagination, so different from the discomfort I felt living in the real world, where no one in my family ever seemed happy.

Later, grown-up, searching for some peace of mind, or dealing with illness or loss or temporary defeat, I could always find safe harbor in a world of make-believe where I might imagine myself in the clouds, or dancing on the moon, or talk-ing to animals in their language. Yes, my feet were still tethered to Earth, but my spirit soared with help from my imagination.

That, then, is what escape means to me, not allowing myself to be dragged down by all that is bad and unpleasant. Instead, by willing and dreaming and imagining, we carve out for ourselves a new path of freedom.

We find joy. So no matter how chained you may feel by life's daily struggles, you must remember that you have the power to become an escape artist and throw off your bindings. Such escapes, sometimes lasting only a few seconds, renew us. They give us the strength to carry on our life's journey. And often in these daydream flights, if we're lucky and if we escape well, we may find the solutions to our problems and obtain our full freedom.

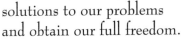

Escape through imagination, through faith and hope is the way to transform pain and hardship into strength and healing. Escape artists do not sit back and allow life to hurt them; instead, first by dreams and then by will and work, they shape their lives into something better. The best way to escape is to journey within one's soul and heart to discover what one feels and wants. This book will help you do just that.

The pages that follow will show you how great escape artists live their lives imaginatively, and, in turn, will encourage you to write, color, draw, and plan your own escapes. To guide you, each page sparks a new thought or idea for you. Answering the question will help you express some of the feelings and thoughts that may have been locked within you and spark your own creativity. You may be surprised by what you learn about yourself. Feel free to add your own doodles, drawings,  or color to the illustrations already in this book. The more you write and draw in this book, the more you make it yours.

You will also find places marked "Escape Clauses" for you to fill in and safely test out your own escapes. There also are "Escape Hatches" with simple suggestions to bring more fun to your life. As you write, draw, or color on these pages, play and have fun and explore what is in your heart. After all, it is only through such explorations that we come to understand ourselves and make new discoveries. And, by the way, it's OK to make mistakes or cross out—nothing you write on this book's pages has to be perfect. Whatever you write or draw is allowed, as long as you try your best to be honest with yourself.

Most importantly, this little book gives you permission to change your life for the better. There is no reason why you need to remain endlessly trapped by your situation. Even if you are a prisoner in a cell—one of your own making or one imposed upon you—you have every right and the freedom to look within your heart and break out through your imagination and your dreams. You really can sprout wings to fly!

Sometimes, escape can be a simple act of reading a wonderful book, or singing a song like a country singer, or licking an ice cream cone with someone you love. Other times, escape means allowing yourself the freedom to dream fervently and hope deeply. Do whatever it takes to throw off your chains before you run out of air. To help you, use the pages marked "A Step to Freedom" to think about the steps you need to take for yourself to find your way free. The steps offered in this book are ones that I have climbed in my own life. There is even space for you to write your own steps. Trust what you know.

And because every escape artist needs from time to time a place to come home to in order to rest and regroup, you will also find within this book "Safe Haven" pages. These will show you how to create special, secure places for yourself and others. They will offer you moments of peace. There are also connect-the-dots pages where with the help of a sharp pencil you will make some wonderful discoveries as you fill in the lines. They will take you to some of the places and things I have searched for in my own imagination. Connect the dots the way you did as a child, filling in your coloring books, eager to see what pictures would emerge.

Lastly, dear reader, you should know that in calling upon my own imagination to write this book I, too, was able to overcome some of the pains in my life. I was able to subvert them and transform them into energy that got me through my days with greater zest and courage. May this happen to you, too. Come to this book's pages when you need to refresh yourself and feed your soul. Engage with this book passionately, and your freed spirit will climb and soar and soar!

Bill Zimmerman

And now, begin . . .

I

What Escape Artists Do

Connect the dots to discover.

*I know a place
where I can walk
on beautiful colors . . .*

≥ ESCAPE ARTISTS ≥

. . . search for butterflies
in unexpected places;
they know these creatures
are waiting to be discovered.

║║║ MY TURN NOW . . . ≥

This is the wish I will make next time I see a butterfly:

(write here)

_____

_____

_____

_____

_____

_____

4

Name a new star: _____

ESCAPE
CLAUSE

_____

_____

_____

ESCAPE ARTISTS

. . . know how to make
every day a Sunday.

Su Mo Tu W Th Fr Sa

▐ ║║║ MY TURN NOW . . . ⟩━━━━▷

The happiest Sunday I well remember was:

ESCAPE
HATCH

Remember someone you love.

ESCAPE ARTISTS

. . . place flowers in their letters
before sealing the envelope
to make someone's life brighter;
a garden unfolds as a letter is opened.

|||| MY TURN NOW . . .

**The letter I have always hoped to receive
has these words in it:**

ESCAPE CLAUSE

Recall a smell that makes you feel safe and cared for—what is it?

_____

_____

_____

ESCAPE ARTISTS

. . . imagine themselves swimming
with pink dolphins and being nuzzled
by these heavenly creatures.

│││││ MY TURN NOW . . . ✎⟩

This is what I think this experience
would be like and how it would change me:

ESCAPE HATCH

Walk by the ocean.

Use your imagination as fully as you can in achieving your goals. Unleashing this power will allow you to think of new possibilities and plan new escape routes. Don't restrict yourself with old ways of thinking. Trust your gut.

▌▌▌▌ MY OWN STEP TO FREEDOM . . .

ESCAPE ARTISTS

. . . at the end of a long day
can still smell
the clean, fresh morning air.

▌▌▌ MY TURN NOW . . . ✎

These are the words I call upon during
the day to keep me steady.

_____

_____

_____

_____

_____

_____

Go
ON

ESCAPE
CLAUSE

You have power to make the world a little better, to make life a bit sweeter.
What would you do? _____

... can reclaim their lost childhood
by playing with a child.

| IIII MY TURN NOW ... >

There is a moment in my own youth I
wish to recapture:

ESCAPE
HATCH

Sing, yodel, and whistle
(all at the same time).

ESCAPE ARTISTS

. . . can leap over
tall buildings
in their imagination.

──────────────────────

|||| MY TURN NOW . . .

**This is the Super Act that deep down I
wish to perform:**

_____

_____

_____

_____

_____

_____

(You can draw on the other side of this page.)

Draw here.

ESCAPE CLAUSE

Applaud yourself for something special you did. What was it?

_____

_____

_____

ESCAPE ARTISTS

. . . can plumb the depths
of the ocean just by gazing
into a fish bowl.

⬛⬛⬛ MY TURN NOW . . . ✏️⟶

The movie scene or painting that I have
always wanted to step into is:

ESCAPE HATCH

Breathe slowly, deeply.

Connect the dots to discover.

*At the ocean,
watching the waves,
I marvel at
these creatures
swimming in the
deep . . .*

Once I walked in a garden and saw a creature with phantasmagorical colors. When she spread her wings it was as if paradise opened to me . . .

Be willful in pursuing your escape.
Be stubborn. Be unbending.
You will need all your grit
to reach your goal.

| ‖‖‖ MY OWN STEP TO FREEDOM . . . ▷ |

ESCAPE ARTISTS

. . . can recapture
a forgotten
memory
just by
sniffing
a smell.

▪▪▪▪ MY TURN NOW . . . ✎

One of my favorite memory smells is:

Go ON

ESCAPE
CLAUSE

Rewrite the opening lines of your life:

_____
_____
_____

ESCAPE ARTISTS

. . . always hug their pets.

MY TURN NOW . . .

This is how I feel when I embrace or pet my own special creature:

ESCAPE HATCH

Visit a pet shop.

ESCAPE ARTISTS

. . . always keep
a fresh box
of crayons
handy
to color
their days.

▮▮▮▮ MY TURN NOW . . . ⟩━━▷

**The drawing that I have always wanted
to make is filled with:**

_____

_____

_____

_____

_____

(You can draw on the other side of this page.)

Go
ON

Draw here.

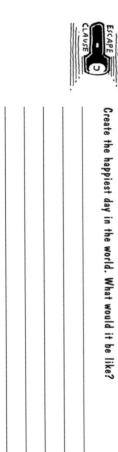

ESCAPE CLAUSE

Create the happiest day in the world. What would it be like?

ESCAPE ARTISTS

. . . can create sonnets
in their minds
and string quartets
in their souls.

|||| MY TURN NOW . . .

The poem I'd write would speak of:

Go on

ESCAPE
HATCH

Listen to a seashell.

ESCAPE ARTISTS

. . . ignore the phone and send
out messages with their minds.

MY TURN NOW . . .

This is the message I would beam
throughout the universe:

_____

_____

_____

_____

_____

_____

Go ON

Name a new cloud: _____

_____

_____

_____

*Think positively. . . . Banish all
negative thoughts. You can't afford
to have bad thoughts deterring you
in your freedom quest.*

▎▎▎ MY OWN STEP TO FREEDOM . . . ▷	

_____

_____

_____

_____

37

ESCAPE ARTISTS

. . . scan the heavens,
waiting to see angels or even E.T.
They always search the horizon
for rainbows or a spaceship.

▨▨▨ MY TURN NOW . . . ▷

This is how I would feel in the presence of angels:

〜〜〜〜〜〜〜〜〜〜〜〜〜〜〜〜〜〜
〜〜〜〜〜〜〜〜〜〜〜〜〜〜〜〜〜〜
〜〜〜〜〜〜〜〜〜〜〜〜〜〜〜〜〜〜
〜〜〜〜〜〜〜〜〜〜〜〜〜〜〜〜〜〜
〜〜〜〜〜〜〜〜〜〜〜〜〜〜〜〜〜〜
〜〜〜〜〜〜〜〜〜〜〜〜〜〜〜〜〜〜

GO ON

ESCAPE HATCH

A.C.

Hug your dog or cat.

ESCAPE ARTISTS

. . . fight pain with laughter
and funny jokes—they pick up
smiles on the streets.

IIII MY TURN NOW . . .

There is someone whom I would like to
make laugh heartily, and this is a funny memory
I can recall:

_____

_____

_____

_____

GO ON

ESCAPE CLAUSE

A cow can produce any flavor milk or juice you like. What flavor would you milk?

_____

_____

ESCAPE ARTISTS

. . . never fail to find the wee chink
of light in a dark room.

|||| MY TURN NOW . . . >

Two things I can do to let light into my own life:

Go son

ESCAPE HATCH

Plant some seeds.

43

ESCAPE ARTISTS

. . . never forget that there are
pixies waiting to be seen.

▐▋▊ MY TURN NOW . . . ✎➤

**Here's what I would say to a leprechaun
or fairy if I were lucky enough to meet one:**

_____
_____
_____
_____
_____

44

ESCAPE CLAUSE

You meet the love of your life—what's he, she, it like?

Connect the dots to discover.

*A*t night when I look up into the heavens, the stars hold a secret message for me . . .

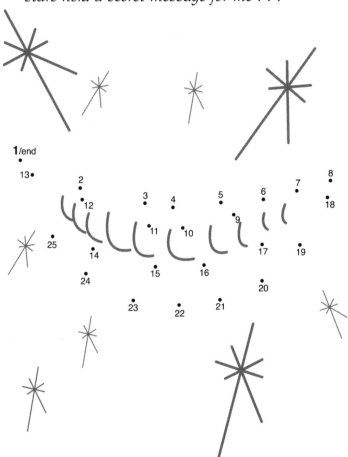

I bring my love a very special bouquet . . .

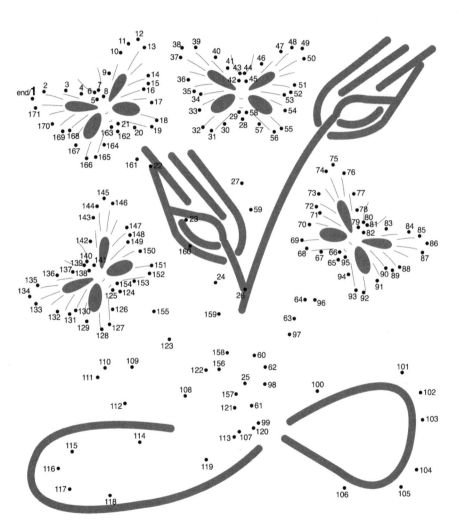

ECHO

*Listen for the music inside
you. . . . It will grow louder as
you near your goal. In your
quest for freedom there will be
times when you should do,
and not think. Sing the song
you know. Be what you are.
Be yourself fully.*

| | |MY OWN STEP TO FREEDOM . . .

_____

_____

_____

_____

ESCAPE ARTISTS

... know in their hearts that they are protected by the spirits of people who loved them.

MY TURN NOW ...

Someone who always made me feel loved and protected:

Go On

ESCAPE HATCH

Watch a Charlie Chaplin or Marx Brothers movie.

ESCAPE ARTISTS

. . . can imagine what it must feel like
to bathe in rose petals.

MY TURN NOW . . .

Someone who loves me enough to prepare
such a wonderful, healing bath:

_____

_____

_____

_____

_____

ESCAPE HATCH

Go fly a kite.

ESCAPE ARTISTS

. . . know what animal they would transform
themselves into if they had the power.

⌐IIII MY TURN NOW . . . ⟩

This is the animal I'd choose to be:

ESCAPE HATCH

Listen to your favorite music.

ESCAPE ARTISTS

. . . can imagine life on distant planets.

▐▐▐▐ MY TURN NOW . . .

These are the words I'd use to greet an alien:

ESCAPE CLAUSE

Plant a 2,000-year-old seed. What will it yield?

ESCAPE ARTISTS

. . . listen intently for the song of the nightingale.

|||| MY TURN NOW . . .

This is the song within me waiting to come out:

Go On

ESCAPE HATCH

Go for a swim.

ESCAPE ARTISTS

. . . know when it is time
to toss off their cares
and cross over into new waters.

▮▯▯ MY TURN NOW . . . ▷

What I'd hope to find on the other side:

_____
_____
_____
_____
_____
_____

ESCAPE CLAUSE

Design a new flower bulb. What is it called? _____

Draw here.

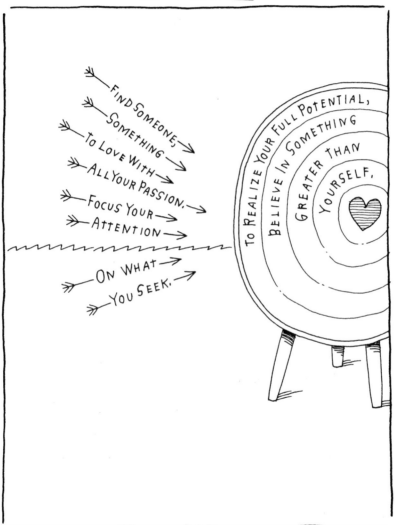

*Find someone, something to love
with all your passion. Focus your
attention on what you seek.
To realize your full potential,
believe in something greater
than yourself.*

IIII MY OWN STEP TO FREEDOM . . .

_____

_____

_____

_____

ESCAPE ARTISTS

. . . can explore new worlds simply by sitting in the quiet of their kitchens and listening to their souls speak.

IIII MY TURN NOW . . .

This is a fine thought or vision I had one morning while sitting quietly at my kitchen table:

_____

_____

_____

_____

(You can draw on the other side of this page.)

Draw here.

Ride your bike.

ESCAPE ARTISTS

. . . write letters to God
in which they share their travails
as well as hopes and joys.

MY TURN NOW . . .

This is a joy and blessing which I thank
God for:

_____

_____

_____

_____

_____

_____

Go on

_____
_____
_____
_____
_____
_____
_____
_____
_____
_____
_____
_____
_____
_____
_____
_____
_____
_____
_____
_____
_____
_____
_____
_____
_____
_____

ESCAPE CLAUSE

Create a new dish: _____
_____
_____
_____

. . . while riding in a crowded commuter train
tap into their dreams
and can imagine themselves
going up the mighty Amazon.

⬚ IIII MY TURN NOW . . . ⟩

**A daydream I had once while riding on
a train or when I was stuck in traffic:**

ESCAPE HATCH

Pray.

ESCAPE ARTISTS

. . . never ever lose hope
when the ground
opens up under their feet.
They know
that somehow,
someday,
things will
get better.

|||| MY TURN NOW . . .

A time when I found the resources and
strength within me to overcome a pressing problem:

_____

_____

_____

_____

ESCAPE CLAUSE

Write a psalm celebrating what is holy in life:

_____

_____

_____

Connect the dots to discover.

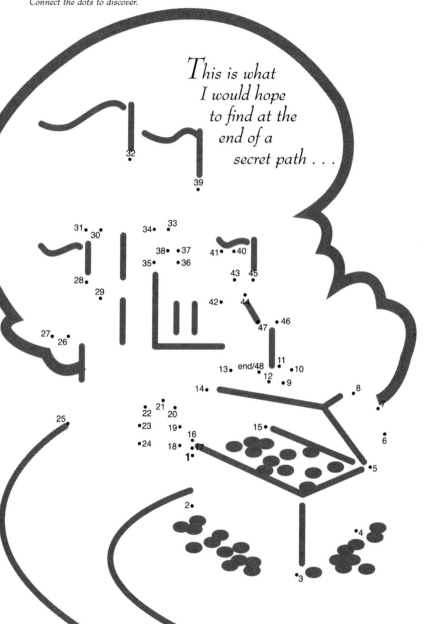

*T*his is what
*I would hope
to find at the
end of a
secret path . . .*

*My little animal friend gives me love
—with no strings attached . . .*

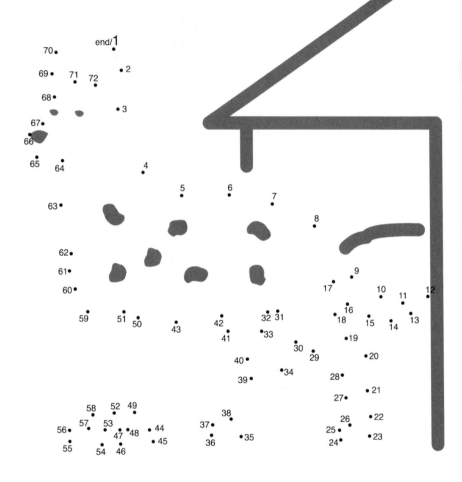

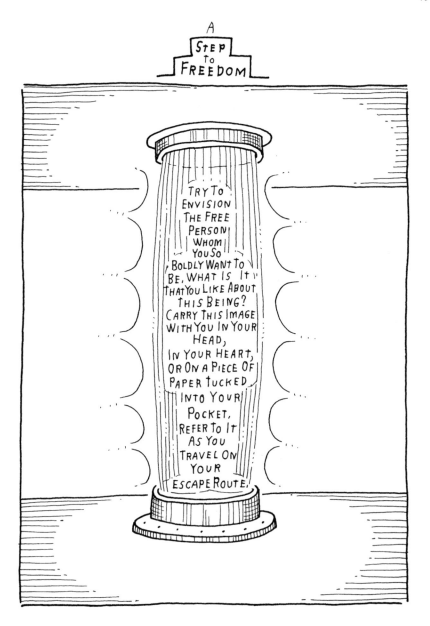

ECHO

*Try to envision the free person
whom you so boldly want to be.
What is it that you like
about this being?
Carry this image with you
in your head, in your heart,
or on a piece of paper
tucked into your pocket.
Refer to it as you travel
on your escape route.*

IIII MY OWN STEP TO FREEDOM . . .

... instinctively know that when
Monday morning comes
they must remember the good times
they have had and will continue to have
in the future.

| III MY TURN NOW ... ▷

The greatest day of my life so far was when:

ESCAPE
HATCH

Attend a play.

ESCAPE ARTISTS

. . . seek to come together with another
human being to ward off the
loneliness of a dark winter night.

MY TURN NOW . . .

**Someone whom I have loved with all my
heart and soul:**

_____

_____

_____

_____

_____

_____

Go ON

Reinvent yourself as: _____

ESCAPE CLAUSE

ESCAPE ARTISTS

. . . know that we can metamorphose
into someone greater
than we are now.

IIII MY TURN NOW . . .

How I want to change:

Go ON

ESCAPE HATCH

Smell a forest in a leaf.

ESCAPE ARTISTS

. . . always dream what's impossible—
they know that somewhere, somehow, some way,
there is "something" better.

MY TURN NOW . . .

An "impossible" dream that I can make come true in my imagination:

_____

_____

_____

_____

_____

_____

Go ON

_____

_____

_____

_____

_____

_____

_____

_____

_____

_____

_____

_____

_____

_____

_____

_____

_____

_____

_____

_____

_____

_____

Design a tattoo: _____

ESCAPE CLAUSE

_____

_____

_____

······· ESCAPE ARTISTS ·······

. . . believe in miracles
and await surprises.

▭▏▏▏▏ MY TURN NOW . . . ▷

A miracle I hope for:

~~~~~~~~~~~~~~~~~~~~~~~~~~
~~~~~~~~~~~~~~~~~~~~~~~~~~
~~~~~~~~~~~~~~~~~~~~~~~~~~
~~~~~~~~~~~~~~~~~~~~~~~~~~
~~~~~~~~~~~~~~~~~~~~~~~~~~
~~~~~~~~~~~~~~~~~~~~~~~~~~

Fantasize.

ESCAPE HATCH

ESCAPE ARTISTS

. . . know that their tears
will feed new growth.

MY TURN NOW . . .

These are the seeds my tears water, and this
is the flower or fruit I hope will emerge:

86

ESCAPE CLAUSE

Name a new day of the week:

To become a great escape artist
you must practice, practice, practice,
with your mind as well as your body.
Rehearse all the things that you will
need to do to get to where you want
to be. Slowly, your talent will grow.
A strong mental game helps you
achieve a great performance.

|||| MY OWN STEP TO FREEDOM . . .

ESCAPE ARTISTS

. . . are always constructing wings
with which to fly.

||||| MY TURN NOW . . .

Where I'd fly away to:

ESCAPE HATCH

A.C.

Do good work.

ESCAPE ARTISTS

. . . can gaze at a weed-filled lot
and discover a garden of Eden.

—————— MY TURN NOW . . . ——▷

**This is how my private garden of Eden
would be:**

_____

_____

_____

_____

_____

(You can draw on the other side of this page.)

Go
on

Draw here.

ESCAPE CLAUSE

Rename yourself: _____

ESCAPE ARTISTS

. . . can look up at the sky
and see clouds of joy.

|||| MY TURN NOW . . .

This is a shape I'd like to see in the clouds:

(You can draw on the other side of this page.)

Go ON

Draw here.

Imagine yourself differently.

ESCAPE ARTISTS

. . . can create comic books
in their heads.

MEANWHILE...

| IIII MY TURN NOW . . .

The superhero whom I always wanted to be:

_____

_____

_____

_____

_____

_____

(You can draw on the other side of this page.)

GO ON

Draw here.

ESCAPE
CLAUSE

Name a new tune: _____

_____

_____

_____

Connect the dots to discover.

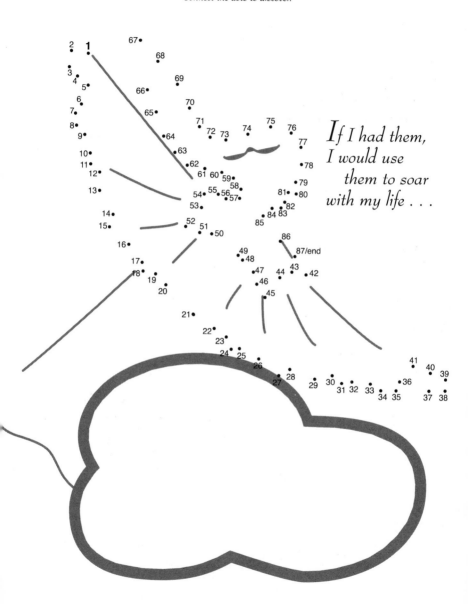

If I had them, I would use them to soar with my life . . .

*T*his is what
  I would like to discover
    at the top of a mountain . . .

A Step to Freedom

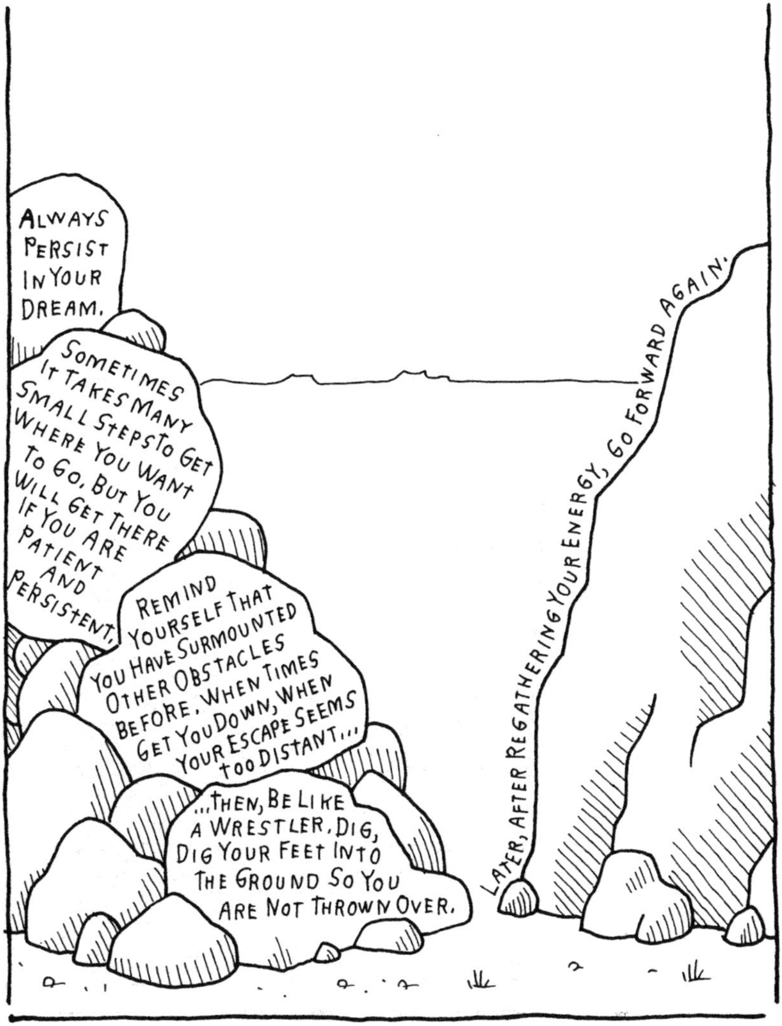

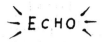

Always persist in your dream. Sometimes it takes many small steps to get where you want to go. But you will get there if you are patient and persistent. Remind yourself that you have surmounted other obstacles before. When times get you down, when your escape seems too distant, then be like a wrestler. Dig, dig your feet into the ground so you are not thrown over. Later, after regathering your energy, go forward again.

MY OWN STEP TO FREEDOM . . .

ESCAPE ARTISTS

. . . surround themselves
with family and loving pets.

IIII MY TURN NOW . . .

My very happiest family memory:

ESCAPE HATCH

Play.

ESCAPE ARTISTS

. . . while sitting in the hidden dark
of the movies become their true selves.

IIII MY TURN NOW . . .

The movie that I make up in my own head:

ESCAPE CLAUSE

Invent an imaginary new friend:

ESCAPE ARTISTS

. . . can listen to the band play
"Let's Face the Music and Dance"
and know that Fred Astaire and Ginger Rogers
lurk within their beings waiting to dance and twirl.

IIII MY TURN NOW . . .

This is the secret person (or even creature) who lurks within my own being:

(You can draw on the other side of this page.)

Draw here.

 **Draw.**

ESCAPE ARTISTS

. . . have learned by now that in walking
in the park, or hearing a bird's song,
or feeling a breeze on their face
they have had a special blessing
bestowed upon them.

IIII MY TURN NOW . . .

This is the blessing I would give to another:

_____

_____

_____

_____

_____

_____

Go ON

ESCAPE CLAUSE

Create a new national holiday: _____

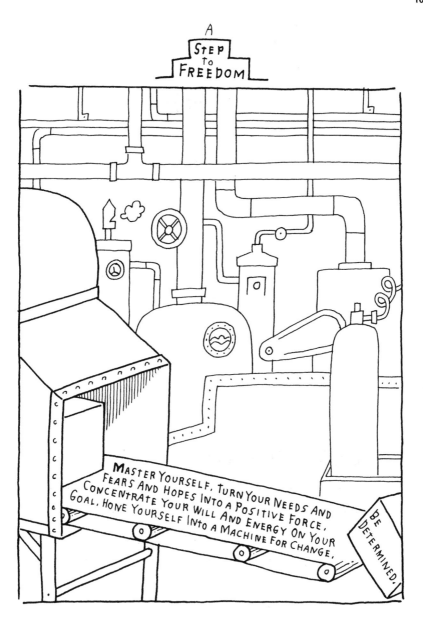

Master yourself.
Turn your needs and fears and
hopes into a positive force.
Concentrate your will
and energy on your goal.
Hone yourself into a machine
for change. Be determined.

||||| MY OWN STEP TO FREEDOM . . . ▷

_____

_____

_____

_____

ESCAPE ARTISTS

... can find safety and love
while holding a puppy or kitten
or feeding a parakeet.

◄ |||| MY TURN NOW ... ▷

There is one animal I'd like to talk to
in its language and this is what I'd ask it:

_____

_____

_____

_____

Ride a camel past the Sphinx.

ESCAPE HATCH

ESCAPE ARTISTS

. . . are thankful for any good luck
that comes their way.

IIII MY TURN NOW . . .

**The luckiest thing that ever happened
to me:**

_____
_____
_____
_____
_____
_____

Go ON

114

Your dream:

ESCAPE CLAUSE

ESCAPE ARTISTS

. . . search for what is holy
in the simple pleasures
of everyday life.

 MY TURN NOW . . .

These are the things or people that
make me feel safe and secure:

GO ON

Putter around with your plants.

ESCAPE
HATCH

ESCAPE ARTISTS

. . . know they can discover
the wonders of the universe
in a tiny library.

▯▯▯▯ MY TURN NOW . . . ✏️

The book that opened the world to me:

ESCAPE CLAUSE

Invent a toy that's fun:

ESCAPE ARTISTS

. . . know how to
scale the walls
when backed into a corner.

||||| MY TURN NOW . . . ▷

A time when I overcame danger:

ESCAPE
HATCH

Make love.

Connect the dots to discover.

I wandered into a new land and hoped to discover this celestial being . . .

It has been said that before we are born we are spirits that can take any shape or form we want. This is the form I would like to assume . . .

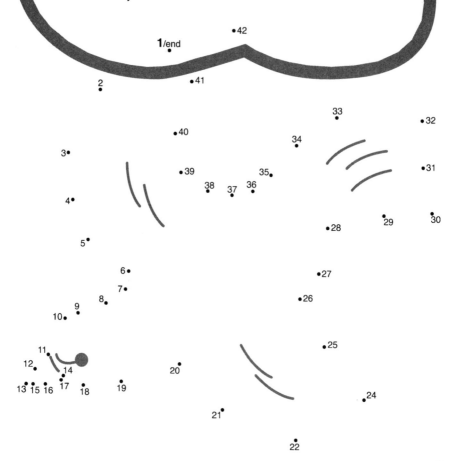

⇒ ECHO ⇐

*Be loose in undertaking
your escape. Break some rules.
Think out of left field.
Stop worrying about
what others will say.
Listen only to that little voice inside
you cheering you on.
It knows best.*

| ||| MY OWN STEP TO FREEDOM . . . ⇒

_____

_____

_____

_____

ESCAPE ARTISTS

. . . can take the bundles of pain
thrown into their lives
and transform them into something better.

▨▨▨ MY TURN NOW . . . ✏

**This is what I learned from illness and
how I changed:**

_____

_____

_____

_____

_____

_____

ESCAPE CLAUSE

Create a new wonder of the world: _____

ESCAPE ARTISTS

. . . always find a way to carry on,
no matter how difficult
the road is under their feet.
They learn to fly instead.

||| MY TURN NOW . . .

A time when I felt like I was floating on air:

Go on

Eat a crisp apple, peel a grape.

ESCAPE ARTISTS

. . . can visualize the flowers
that will bloom
when they plant the seeds.

MY TURN NOW . . .

The sight of this flower always has thrilled me:

_____

_____

_____

_____

_____

_____

(You can draw on the other side of this page.)

Go
On

Draw here.

ESCAPE
CLAUSE

Name a newborn baby:

ESCAPE ARTISTS

. . . can laugh with amazement
at the folly of their lives
and all that they have survived.

|||| MY TURN NOW . . .

I laugh with glee when I think back to
the time when:

~~~~~~~~~~~~~~~~~~

~~~~~~~~~~~~~~~~~~

~~~~~~~~~~~~~~~~~~

~~~~~~~~~~~~~~~~~~

~~~~~~~~~~~~~~~~~~

~~~~~~~~~~~~~~~~~~

ESCAPE HATCH

Hope.

A
STEP
TO
FREEDOM

AN ESCAPE ARTIST NEEDS A STRONG BODY AND VAST RESERVES OF ENERGY TO BREAK APART SHACKLES.

CARE FOR YOUR BODY AND GOOD HEALTH AS CAREFULLY AND LOVINGLY AS YOU WOULD YOUR SOUL.

An escape artist needs
a strong body and vast reserves
of energy to break apart shackles.
Care for your body and good health
as carefully and lovingly as you
would your soul.

⬛ **MY OWN STEP TO FREEDOM . . .**

_____

_____

_____

_____

ESCAPE ARTISTS

. . . can walk the tightrope of life
without falling off into the abyss.
They steady themselves
with prayer and hope and skill.

▏▏▏▏ MY TURN NOW . . . ✎

A circus act I would like to perform:

(You can draw on the other side of this page.) **GO ON**

ESCAPE CLAUSE

Something new I wish to learn:

_____

_____

Draw here.

ESCAPE ARTISTS

. . . can make up wondrous stories watching the clouds move across the sky.

|||| MY TURN NOW . . .

A story I would make up for a child:

ESCAPE HATCH

Recall a happy moment.

ESCAPE ARTISTS

. . . reach into the past and transform
all its pain and hurt
into wisdom and growth.

▐▐▐▐ MY TURN NOW . . . ✎

If I had a magic wand, this is what I would change:

_____

_____

_____

_____

_____

(You can draw on the other side of this page.)

140

Draw here.

ESCAPE
CLAUSE

Test a sixth sense:

ESCAPE ARTISTS

. . . know there is music
within their souls
that can rival
a Bach cantata
or mimic the sounds
of the celestial spheres.

▌▌▌ MY TURN NOW . . .

A singer I'd love to hear croon to me and the song I'd want to hear sung would be:

Go on

Find comfort in the lap
of someone you love.

ESCAPE
HATCH

Connect the dots to discover.

When I was little and read many stories about ancient peoples, I used to think of a magical, faraway place where this creature could be found . . .

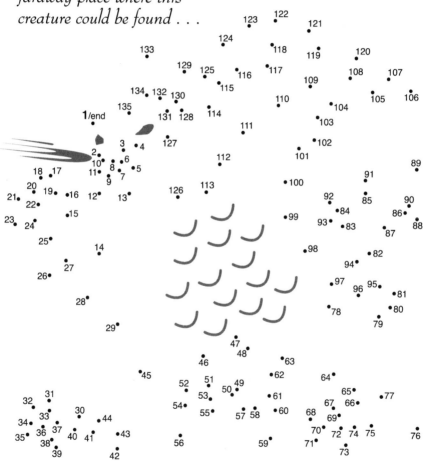

If I could walk
on the bottom
of the sea, here
is a creature I
would hope to
play with . . .

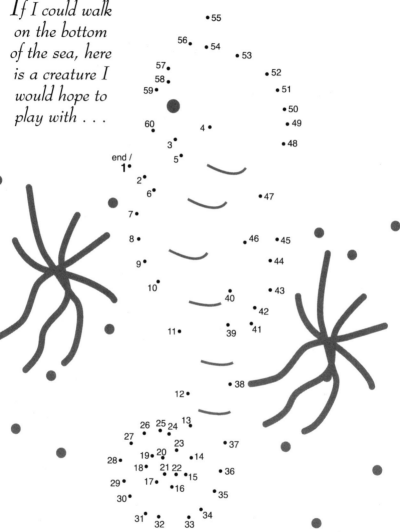

ECHO

Throw fear to the winds.
You must be brave like a lion
to withstand the rigors
of your undertaking.
Courage is within you.
Call upon it. Insist on it.
Roar when you need to.

||||| MY OWN STEP TO FREEDOM . . .

_____

_____

_____

_____

ESCAPE ARTISTS

... can look into their souls
and always find the nuggets of gold
that lay hidden within.

MY TURN NOW ...

A good deed done to me for which I can never place a high enough price:

_____
_____
_____
_____
_____
_____

_____
_____
_____
_____
_____
_____
_____
_____
_____
_____
_____
_____
_____
_____
_____
_____
_____
_____
_____
_____
_____
_____
_____
_____

ESCAPE CLAUSE

Your hope: _____
_____
_____
_____

 **ESCAPE ARTISTS**

. . . are always open to the mystery
and excitement of life.

IIII MY TURN NOW . . .

A trick or skill I'd like to learn:

~~~~~~

~~~~~~

~~~~~~

~~~~~~

~~~~~~

~~~~~~

GO ON

Create a new superhero.

ESCAPE
HATCH

ESCAPE ARTISTS

. . . remain ever youthful
even when they grow old.

| IIII MY TURN NOW . . . ⟩

What I'd like to be able to do or achieve
by the time I'm 100:

ESCAPE
CLAUSE

Transform yourself into a:

_____

_____

ESCAPE ARTISTS

. . . may move slow as snails, but in their mind
they still win the race,
overcoming their own limits.

IIII MY TURN NOW . . . >

A mountain in my life that I hope to scale:

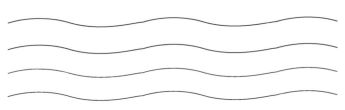

ESCAPE HATCH

Take a bubble bath.

A
STEP
TO
FREEDOM

IN MAKING YOUR ESCAPE, ALWAYS CLING TENACIOUSLY TO HOPE; DO NOT ALLOW YOUR FINGERS TO BE PRIED AWAY. HOPE AND IMAGINATION ARE THE VERY THINGS THAT ALLOW YOU TO SOAR.

In making your escape,
always cling tenaciously to hope;
do not allow your
fingers to be pried away.
Hope and imagination are the very
things that allow you to soar.

|||| MY OWN STEP TO FREEDOM . . .

ESCAPE ARTISTS

. . . can find the light even when
darkness descends upon them.

IIII MY TURN NOW . . .

**A sight or experience that always
brightens my life:**

_____
_____
_____
_____
_____

(You can draw on the other side of this page.)

Draw here.

ESCAPE CLAUSE

Name your own island:

_____

ESCAPE ARTISTS

. . . always believe
in flying carpets
and the power of wishing.

IIII MY TURN NOW . . .

**Three wishes I would make if I could
rub Aladdin's lamp:**

Dream of Sunday on Monday.

ESCAPE ARTISTS

. . . build escalators to heaven
in their minds.

MY TURN NOW . . .

What I hope heaven on earth would be like:

_____
_____
_____
_____
_____
_____

(You can draw on the other side of this page.)

Go On

Draw here.

Discover a new country: ⎯⎯⎯⎯⎯⎯⎯⎯⎯

ESCAPE
CLAUSE

ESCAPE ARTISTS

. . . toss fear to the wind
and are always ready to dip their big toe
into new waters.

▐▐▌ MY TURN NOW . . .

A time, I am proud to say, when I was brave:

~~~~~~

~~~~~~

~~~~~~

~~~~~~

~~~~~~

~~~~~~

GoJON

Practice your comedy routine.

ESCAPE ARTISTS

. . . walk along the shore and become one
with the ocean as it washes over their feet.

IIII MY TURN NOW . . .

How I feel when I am at the ocean:

ESCAPE CLAUSE

Invent a four-footed pet:

_____

_____

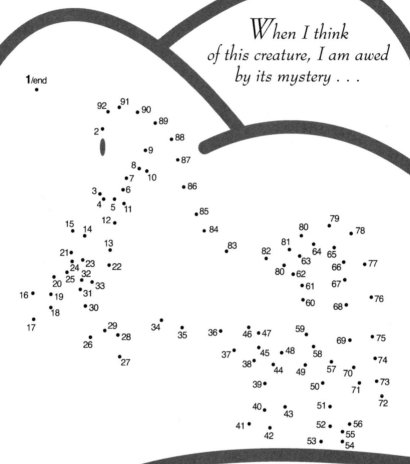

Connect the dots to discover.

When I think of this creature, I am awed by its mystery . . .

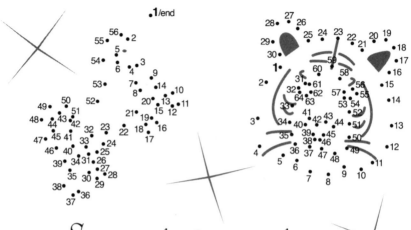

*Sometimes when I gaze up at the stars,
I imagine the most wondrous new constellations.
Here are some of them . . .*

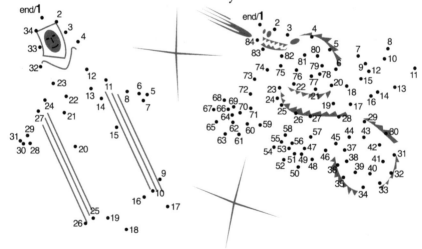

A
STEP
TO
FREEDOM

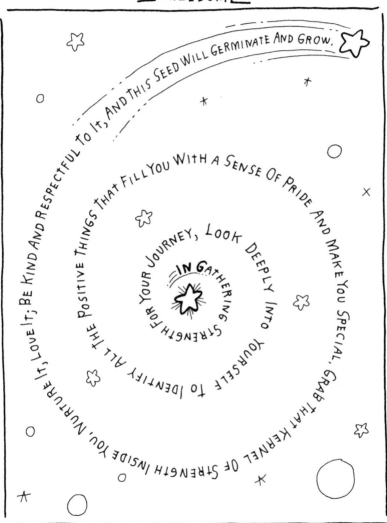

IN Gathering Strength for Your Journey, Look Deeply Into Yourself To Identify All the Positive Things that Fill You With a Sense Of Pride And Make You Special. Grab that Kernel Of Strength Inside You, Nurture It, Love It; Be Kind And Respectful to It, And This Seed Will Germinate And Grow.

$\searrow$ ECHO $\swarrow$

*In gathering strength for your
journey, look deeply into yourself
to identify all the positive things
that fill you with a sense of pride
and make you special. Grab that
kernel of strength inside you.
Nurture it, love it; be kind and
respectful to it, and this seed will
germinate and grow.*

||||| MY OWN STEP TO FREEDOM . . .

_____

_____

_____

_____

ESCAPE ARTISTS

. . . can transport themselves
out of this world into another
through their powers of imagination.

▌▌▌ MY TURN NOW . . . ▷

**Places that I fly to, people whom I talk
to in my imagination:**

172

Sleep.

ESCAPE ARTISTS

. . . always look for the sun to come out
after the rain stops.

IIII MY TURN NOW . . .

Things I can do to move the clouds in
my life:

_____
_____
_____
_____
_____
_____

ESCAPE CLAUSE

Name the 13th month: _____

ESCAPE ARTISTS

. . . find a way to break out of a cell
not of their own making
through strong will
and good memories.

MY TURN NOW . . .

A time when I broke out of my own prison:

Walk on a bridge of rainbows.

ESCAPE
HATCH

≥ ESCAPE ARTISTS ≥

. . . in their solitude
sing songs and tell stories
to imaginary friends and acquaintances.

▭▯▯ MY TURN NOW . . . ⟩

**An old, old friend whom I'd give anything
to talk with:**

_____

_____

_____

_____

_____

_____

Name a vast ocean: _____

ESCAPE
CLAUSE

*Don't be afraid to reach out to
others so they may help you
along your escape path.
Your connectedness with them
will make your journey less
daunting and less lonely.*

IIII MY OWN STEP TO FREEDOM . . . ⟩▷

ESCAPE ARTISTS

. . . never give up despite
physical shortcomings or illness.

IIII MY TURN NOW . . .

A finish line that I have crossed:

GO
ON

ESCAPE HATCH

Smell fresh-baked bread.

ESCAPE ARTISTS

. . . never walk down the streets
without expecting that a great
discovery or wonderful surprise
will be just around the corner.

IIII MY TURN NOW . . .

A discovery which I still hope to make:

ESCAPE CLAUSE

What would be your nightclub act?

ESCAPE ARTISTS

... believe in butterfly seeds.

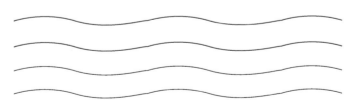

||||| MY TURN NOW ...

Other magical seeds I'd like to grow:

(You can draw on the other side of this page.)

GO ON

Draw here.

ESCAPE HATCH

Talk to the divine

ESCAPE ARTISTS

. . . easily remember what it is like to plop down
in a pile of leaves in the fall
and toss them over their heads.

▐▐▐▐ MY TURN NOW . . . ▷

**A very happy time when I was very
young that I still remember:**

_____

_____

_____

_____

_____

_____

Go
On

188

Write the opening lines of a song:

ESCAPE
CLAUSE

ESCAPE ARTISTS

. . . know exactly what they would do
upon winning the million-dollar lottery.

MY TURN NOW . . .

How I'd use a million bucks:

GO ON

Walk your dog or just yourself.

Connect the dots to discover.

I think of this creature walking the streets of my city . . .

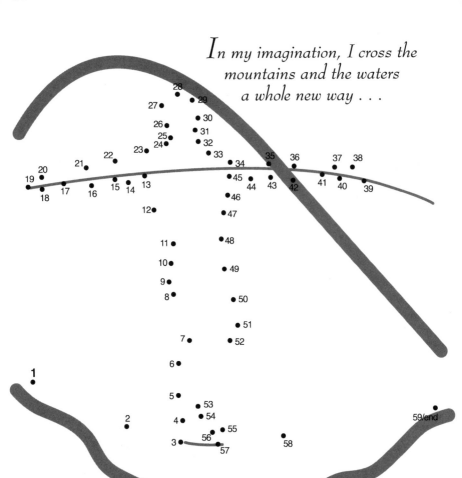

*I*n my imagination, I cross the
mountains and the waters
a whole new way . . .

A
STEP
TO
FREEDOM

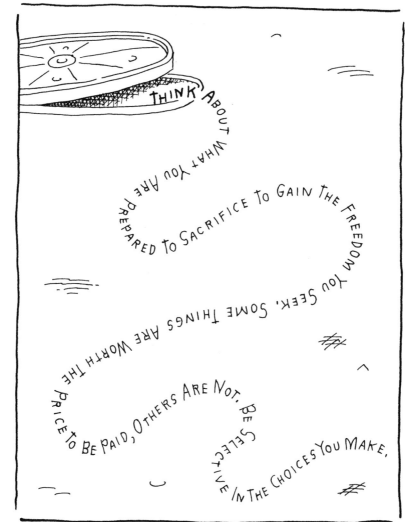

THINK ABOUT WHAT YOU ARE PREPARED TO SACRIFICE TO GAIN THE FREEDOM YOU SEEK. SOME THINGS ARE WORTH THE PRICE TO BE PAID, OTHERS ARE NOT. BE SELECTIVE IN THE CHOICES YOU MAKE.

⊰ ECHO ⊱

*Think about what you
are prepared to sacrifice
to gain the freedom you seek.
Some things are worth
the price to be paid,
others are not.
Be selective in the
choices you make.*

| ▐▌▌MY OWN STEP TO FREEDOM . . . ⟩═▷ |

_____

_____

_____

_____

ESCAPE ARTISTS

. . . can create maps of strange lands
in their heads when feeling trapped.

⊞ MY TURN NOW . . .

A new kingdom I'd like to discover or
an old one I'd like to explore:

_____

_____

_____

_____

_____

_____

Make a vow to yourself: —————

ESCAPE
CLAUSE

ESCAPE ARTISTS

. . . believe that angels hover over
to protect them from harm.

| IIII MY TURN NOW . . . >

The name of the angel who watches over
me is:

~~~~~~~~~~~~~~~~~~~~~~~~
~~~~~~~~~~~~~~~~~~~~~~~~
~~~~~~~~~~~~~~~~~~~~~~~~
~~~~~~~~~~~~~~~~~~~~~~~~
~~~~~~~~~~~~~~~~~~~~~~~~
~~~~~~~~~~~~~~~~~~~~~~~~

Go ON

Search for the Komodo dragon.

ESCAPE ARTISTS

. . . know how to keep their dignity even when bad things happen to them. They know the secret of making the best of what life hands them.

| IIII MY TURN NOW . . . ⟩

The time I transformed an unhappy situation into one of personal growth:

ESCAPE CLAUSE

Name a new ice cream flavor:

ESCAPE ARTISTS

. . . can sometimes hear the grass grow.

| IIII MY TURN NOW . . . >

Things I know that nobody else knows:

202

ESCAPE HATCH

R.C.

Buy a toy.

ESCAPE ARTISTS

. . . always carry their bags
of dreams with them.

▐ ||| MY TURN NOW . . . ⊏▷

Some joyful dreams in my bag:

_____

_____

_____

_____

_____

_____

(You can draw on the other side of this page.)

GO ON

Draw here.

Say all the magic escape words: travel, fly, dance, leap, flow, twirl, soar, burrow, traipse, skip, love.

When you find your freedom—
what then?
Time now to exult in
what you have accomplished.
Do not take for granted how far you
have come or the many perils you
have faced in order to get this far.
Instead, take as much pleasure in
what you've gained as you did in the
pursuit of your dream.

| IIII MY OWN STEP TO FREEDOM . . . ⟩▷ |

_____

_____

_____

_____

ESCAPE ARTISTS

. . . when feeling weak can find strength
in the sounds of a bird's song,
the purr of a kitten,
a wet lick from their dog.

MY TURN NOW . . .

An animal spirit that I'd like to incorporate within me:

ESCAPE HATCH

Encounter the Cat People in the Amazon.

ESCAPE ARTISTS

. . . hear music
when others hear silence.

MY TURN NOW . . .

Music that always calms my soul and transports me to another place:

_____
_____
_____
_____
_____
_____

ESCAPE
CLAUSE

Name your spaceship:

ESCAPE ARTISTS

. . . know how to live
for the thrill of the moment.

| MY TURN NOW . . .

A moment in my life that I will always
cherish and wish I could replicate:

ESCAPE HATCH

AC

Think of a sunset while stuck in traffic.

ESCAPE ARTISTS

. . . can hear a New Orleans jazz band
in the sound of car horns.

▏▎▎ MY TURN NOW . . .

**A song or piece of music that reflects
what I seek in life:**

Remember the sweet smell of a baby, its tiny fingers clutching yours.

ESCAPE ARTISTS

. . . can truly imagine
holding rainbows in their hands.

▭▯▯▯ MY TURN NOW . . . ▷

What it would feel like to hold a rainbow,
or even a cloud or ray of sunshine, and whom I
might share this with:

_____

_____

ESCAPE HATCH

Hear a child's giggle.

Connect the dots to discover.

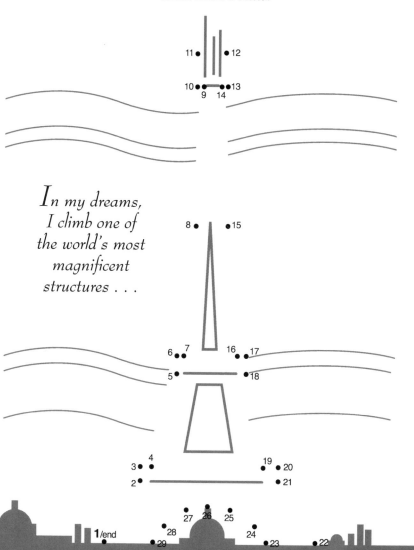

In my dreams, I climb one of the world's most magnificent structures . . .

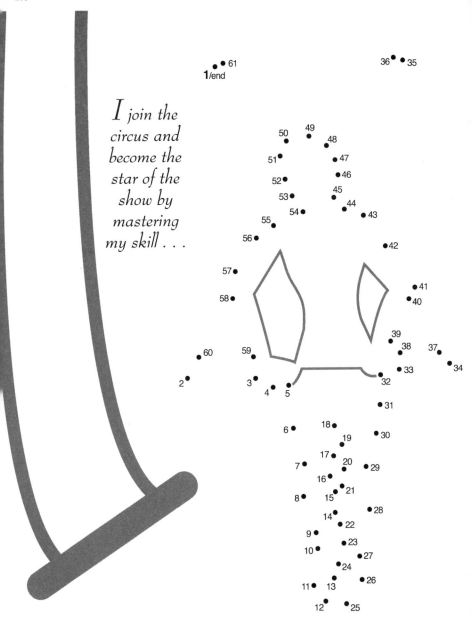

I join the circus and become the star of the show by mastering my skill . . .

ECHO

When you are finally free, embrace the feeling of freedom. Think deeply about how you will use your liberty. With freedom comes responsibility. Reflect on what you have learned along your journey and choose to use part of your new freedom to make the world a better place. You must not close your eyes to the shackles worn by other people. As long as some are still in chains, none of us will ever be fully free.

Go forward now . . .

MY OWN STEP TO FREEDOM . . .
_____
_____
_____
_____

Connect the
dots to discover.

*In India everything looks
spectacular when I travel
around the country with the
help of this magnificent
creature . . .*

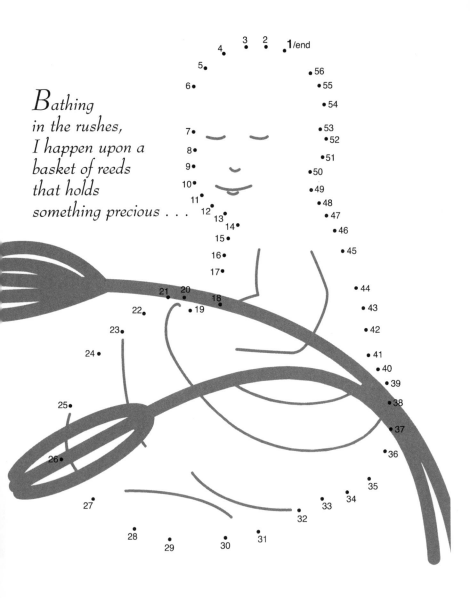

*B*athing
in the rushes,
I happen upon a
basket of reeds
that holds
something precious . . .

Sometimes I imagine that I am rejoined with two special people, and we are united and happy together . . .

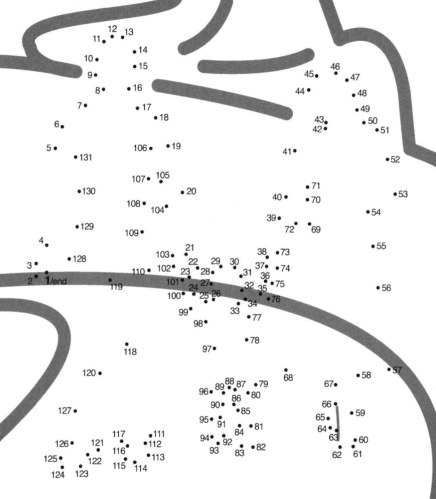

What is a Safe Haven?

A quiet place where you can
search safely for your thoughts
and find them . . .

Every escape artist needs a safe haven.
No matter how successful we are in escaping our
life situation or in surmounting our particular
problem, each of us needs to have a safe home to
return to. After having soared and transported
ourselves, we need a place of refuge in which to
rest and restore ourselves, to catch our breath
before we venture out again.

The image of the bird comes to mind. This
beautiful creature escapes the hunter or famine

 by flying away. It may fly, it may glide, but at some time it will need to touch down for a while before continuing on its journey. It will need to find a safe place to feed and nurture its young.

Are human beings any less different? Through our imaginations, through our will and determination, we too flee from our tormentors or threats to our existence. At some point in our excursions we must find our way back to a home or into the arms of a lover or to a quiet, safe spot. There, we can finally breathe deeply, nourish ourselves, sleep peacefully, and awaken restored. Sometimes this safe haven is a quiet room or church or museum corner. Other times this safe haven is in our hearts —a prayer to God or a memory of something or someone special—maybe even a hope or dream.

I believe that ultimately, the strongest, safest havens are the ones we build from within, piece by piece by tiny piece. If we can't construct our own refuge, then we will be always vulnerable to harsh external elements. No one can provide us with safety but ourselves and our God.

Each morn I struggle in the dark to piece my own soul together. As I sit by my kitchen table, putting down on paper the words to this and other books, I find a way to provide a safe haven for me. My book becomes a place where I allow myself to test the waters of self, to make  mistakes, to play, to explore what is in my heart. My thoughts, my pen and paper, the wonderful quiet of the early morning punctuated by the chirps of a pet bird, my dog by my feet, all provide me with moments of solace. They help me keep the tigers that threaten me at bay. Writing, then, is the only way I know how to protect myself.

Now, ask yourself what special things or people provide safe havens for you? What is your refuge? What are the things that save you and protect you?

How do you build a safe haven? You reach into yourself and search for your core strengths that always reside within and which you can call upon from time to time. With your strengths you construct a space you can crawl into and that can protect you. And in this space you tune into your thoughts to see who you are and what you feel.

As a child I wanted so deeply to have a safe haven. When Friday afternoons came and school was over, I would dread the weekends because I knew my parents would have more time to fight and hurt one another. I knew that books would provide a safe haven for me. So, on Fridays every week I would go to the library, seek out my wonderful librarian, and return home with an armful of golden books to transport me out of a world of uncertainty and fighting into the safer world of imagination.

Just as I found my safe haven, so must you discover your own. They are there, I promise you, if you search intently.

WHAT YOU CAN DO
TO CREATE SAFE HAVENS

It doesn't take much to create a safe haven for
someone. Just provide

— a little love
— a little reassurance
— a hug, an embrace
— an atmosphere that is positive, where the word "no" is
  rarely used
— a place of quiet surroundings of color and beauty
— a home of unselfishness and trust
— goodness and grace
— a sense of God and the holy
— a setting where honesty and truth are encouraged,
  where it is all right to ask questions even if all the
  answers are not found immediately
— a setting where there is no shame and acceptance of
  one's differences is given.

Safe havens are provided by

— music
— sounds of a bird's chirping
— the peace of early morning
— the opportunity to feel and reflect
— having time to wonder and think
— people you love.

You can create safe havens by performing simple acts of hope. Some of these are

- planting seeds and bulbs in memory of those you love and to signify your hopes for the future
- stroking a pet you love and whispering to it all that is in your heart
- walking in a conservatory of butterflies
- lighting memory candles
- gazing up at night at a ceiling of luminescent stars and planets you have pasted there to guide you through the dark
- kneading dough and baking bread or cookies
- coloring with a fresh box of crayons
- watching multitudes of kites flying in the sky
- remembering summer lightning bugs signaling to you in the early summer dusk
- hearing a chorus of children sing
- imagining a cornucopia of food that feeds all the world's hungry
- gazing at children's faces as they learn and the world opens up to them
- watching dolphins leaping and dipping
- talking to an older person to learn how they overcame troubles and asking them to share what wisdom they acquired—you in turn give them your love and friendship
- taking a walk by the sea
- helping others, being a little less selfish.

MY TURN NOW . . .

What acts of hope come to your mind?

_____

_____

_____

_____

_____

_____

_____

_____

_____

_____

_____

_____

_____

_____

_____

_____

_____

_____

_____

_____

SOME SAFE HAVENS ARE

— a place where children can rest and be protected

— a place where the phone doesn't ring with bad news

— a room with a beautifully lit Christmas tree with colors of red and yellow, blue, and green.

— a kitchen table where you do your work

— a land where there is no war

— a small apartment filled with love and color

— a dog or cat who loves you so

— a lover or child whom you protect and who, in turn, safeguards you with their love

— a person who listens to you, who allows you to share what is in your heart and doesn't judge you

— a hill of dazzling daffodils

— a place where there is no fighting or anger

— a place where people respect one another

— an imaginary place deep in your imagination

— a child—a parent's bravest hopes, the being who makes their lives worth living

– a quiet place where you can search safely for your thoughts and find them

– a memory that makes you happy in recalling it

– a dark movie house where you can enter the world of the screen

– a prayer or poem that carries you through

– a cup of fresh coffee in the morning and the sound of beautiful music on the radio.

`| IIII MY TURN NOW . . . >`

What are your own safe havens?

_____

_____

_____

_____

_____

_____

_____

_____

_____

Bye-Byes

Early-Morning Thoughts
of an Escape Artist . . .

(i)

Dawn is here
The day is forming.
What will I be today?
A tiger? A soldier?
A fearful man?
A brave soul?
Will I fall on my face
   or stand steady against
   what troubles me?
Will I do good,
   or will I fail because
   of my selfishness?

(ii)

Dawn has come
The day is forming.
Who will I be today?
A young girl?
A frightened child?
Will I battle once more for my
   life, or will I find a wind of
   peace bathing my body?
Will I do brave deeds?
What will the day call forth in
   me?
What will I pull out from my bag
   of tricks to earn my new day
   of life?

(iii)

Is that a soul I hear?
Is that a babe crying?
Is that the flap of an angel's wings in
   the darkness?
Is that a call I hear, willing me to take
   a leap into the unknown?
But who will pick me up if I stumble?
Can I overcome myself?

ESCAPE QUESTIONS

What is inside of us waiting to escape?

Who is that being within we are waiting to know?

What does the voice sound like whose shout we are waiting
to hear?

What is that dream we wait patiently to experience?

Whose pulse beats within our skin?

What is the deed that needs to be done?

When will we finally hear the music that plays in our
soul?

When will we give birth to the child waiting for its chance
to breathe life?

What can we do to help in the birth of the being we really
want to be?

How do we discard the old skin and breathe the new life
we want to have? Will God help us? Or, do we have to
call on every shard of strength that rests inside us and
pull from our beings the person waiting to be free?

How does one rescue oneself?

How does one escape from one's confinement?

How does one give birth to a new life that has a better
chance to succeed than the old one?

How can I open up like a flower to bloom and to be
splendid?

Or, am I doomed to remain a spore that waits for only
once-in-a-century conditions to finally sprout?

Where does one find the power of life?

I must search within to find all these answers, just as I must find my share of sunlight from within my being. I am no different from any other escape artist who searches for a reason in life.

▌▌▌▌ MY TURN NOW . . . ▷

What will I escape from?

_____

_____

Where will I escape to?

_____

_____

What will I do with my freedom?

_____

_____

Here is space for my own questions or answers:

_____

_____

_____

Space to Write, Think, and Doodle

Space to Write, Think, and Doodle

About This Book's Escape Artists

Bill Zimmerman began writing *Doodles & Daydreams* at a time when his soul was crying. He has authored many books to help people tap into their imaginations to live more fully and creatively. Like this one, his books are interactive to encourage readers to express their deepest thoughts and feelings and to find comfort. They include

Lunch Box Letters, which encourages parents to write notes of love and encouragement to their children;

How to Tape Instant Oral Biographies, a family oral history guide;

A Book of Questions to Keep Thoughts and Feelings, a new form of diary/journal;

Make Beliefs and Make Beliefs for Kids of All Ages, books to spur the imagination and encourage creativity;

Lifelines: A Book of Hope, to get people through hard times;

The Little Book of Joy, a book of prayer and meditation;

DOGMAS: Simple Truths From a Wise Pet (also known as The Dog's Bark) and

CAT-e-CHISMS: Feline Answers to Life's Big Questions (also known as The Cat's Meow), books which communicate the wisdom to be learned from animals;

A Book of Sunshine, which aims to remove the clouds in our lives;

My Life: An Open Book, which helps people write down the wisdom they have learned through their life's experiences;

Idea Catcher for Kids, which helps young people find their writer's voice;

Butterfly Wishes, a journal to write down what is deepest in your heart;

My Paper Memory Quilt, a family activity book to create a paper patchwork quilt that depicts a family's history; and

100 Things Guys Need to Know, a book of encouraging words to help boys as they make their way through life.

For more information about his books, write to:
Bill Zimmerman
Guarionex Press Ltd.
201 West 77 Street
New York, NY 10024
To order by phone: 212-724-5259
E-mail: wmz@aol.com
Visit his Web sites at www.billztreasurechest.com and
www.makebeliefscomix.com

Tom Bloom is an artist who finds an
escape route in every blank piece of paper
that passes across his desk and then some.
Though capable of getting lost in a train of
thought, he easily dreams his way back on
track. Over the years he has plotted a circu-
itous path of periodicals and publications in
the print world. He lives in a small suburb of
New York City with a major family, or vice versa.

Eileen Berasi, who designed this book and created
its connect-the-dots pages, has been a map designer
for twenty-five years. She is the co-founder of
**Graphic Chart & Map Co. Inc., (www.char-
tandmap.com),** specialists in map design, and
mapPoster.com (www.mapPoster.com), a retailer
of the company's award-winning aerial maps of
downtown American cities. The map of her world
includes Hastings-on-Hudson, New York, where
she lives with her husband and three children.

Share With Us

Dear reader,

Please share with us any thoughts you might have in reading and using *Doodles & Daydreams*. We'd also like to hear how you escape through your own imagination. Your comments, suggestions, and questions to make this book even more useful to you are very welcome. If you send us ideas for possible use in future editions of this book, please also give us written permission to use them. We will send you a free copy if an idea is used. Thank you.

Write to:
Bill Zimmerman
Guarionex Press Ltd.
201 West 77 Street
New York, NY 10024
or E-mail to: **wmz@aol.com**
www.billztreasurechest.com
www.makebeliefscomix.com